INDIAN FOLK ART OF BIHAR MADHUBANI PAINTINGS - I

RUCHY JAIN

ISBN 979-888606145-1

In loving memories of

my late father Shri Ashok Jain

Contents

ONE

INTRODUCTION

Madhubani Paintings traditionally done by women of the villages around Madhubani town, started 2500 years ago, are also knnown as Mithila Paintings. The name “Madhubani” means “honey forest”. The art extends to the adjoining parts of Terai region in Nepal.

Geographical Region

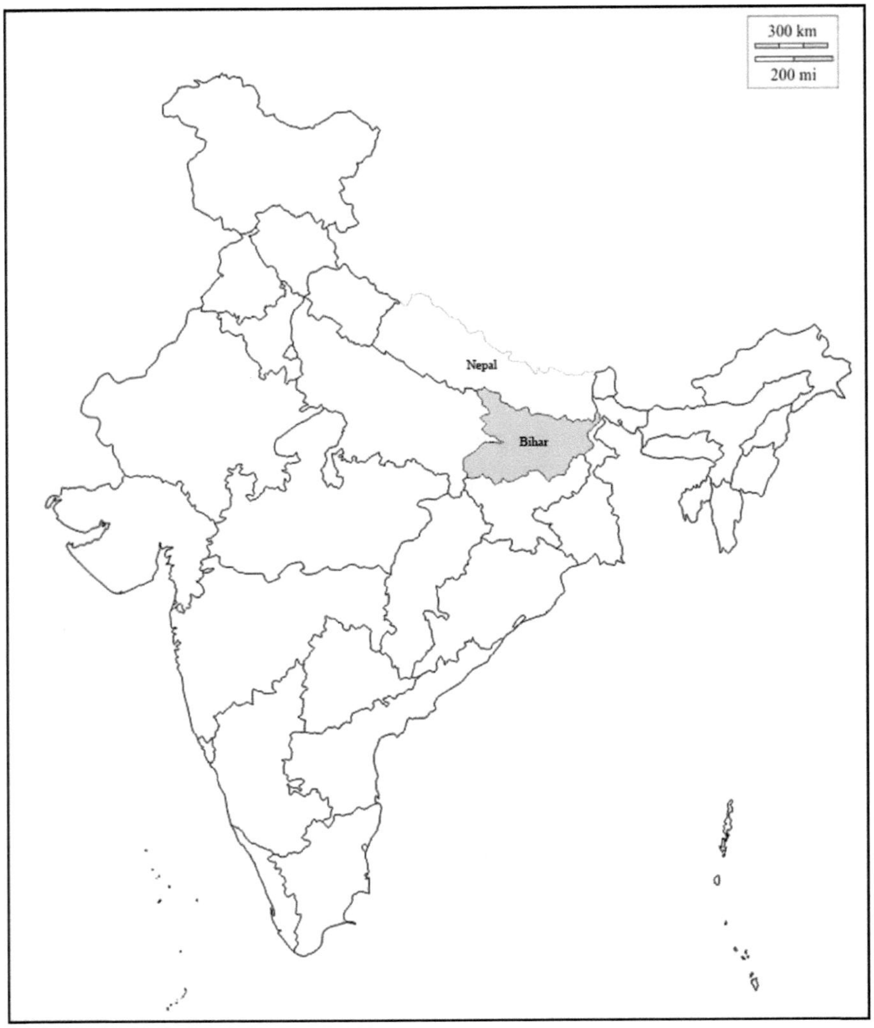

Map Of India showing state of Bihar and Neighbouring Nepal

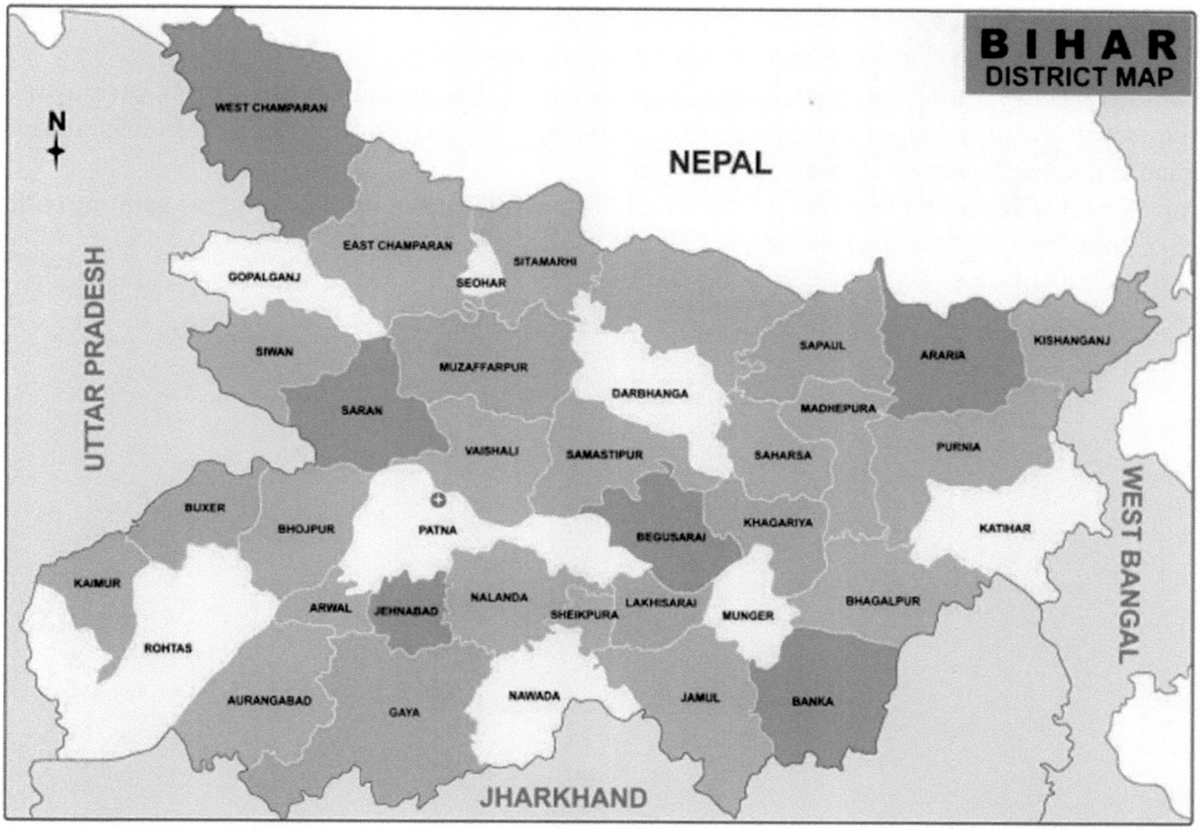

Map Of Bihar, showing Madhubani Town And Tarai Region in Nepal

History

The Origin of Madhubani is believed to be during the period of Ramayan when King Janak of Mithila told people of his kingdom to paint walls and floors of their houses on marriage of Sita and Lord Ram. People believed that doing so pleased the Gods.

Painting Pattern Styles

Madhubani Art has five distinctive styles: Bharni, Kachni, Tantrik, Godna and Kohbar. Bharni, kachni and Tantrik styles themes were mainly religious and they depicted Gods and Goddesses, flora and fauna paintings, and were done by Brahman and Kayasth women, considered "top caste".

Bharni- This art is the most profound art form out of the five. It is known for "filling" of the painting with vibrant and bright colors.

Bharni

Kachni- This art style is made using the monochrome color scheme or only two colors are used to complete the full painting. These paintings come from the Kayastha Community. The distinction in form is mainly the linework of the painting, where there is another line outlining the sketch at a distance and the gap between the two lines is filled with diagonal, straight and curved lines. These lines are also filled throughtout the painting instead of filling colors. These kinds of paintings portray natural aspects, flora and fauna.

Kachni

Tantrik- This art style solely depicts religious texts and characters related to them and includes manifestations of Maha Durga, Maha Saraswati, Maha Lakshmi and Maha Ganesh along with other tantrik symbols. The colors used in this style are the colors that are used in tantric texts and are made for special religious prayers.

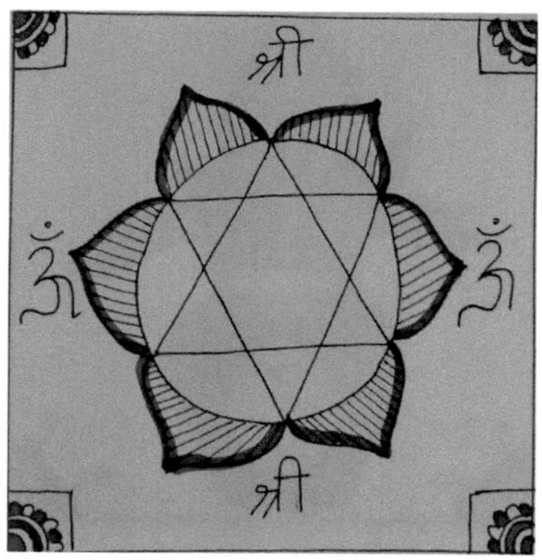

Tantrik

Godna- This art is popularly used by Paswan artists. Godna also known as Tattoo paintings. They are very fine in line, are largely composed of concentric circles and rows of flowers, fields, animals, figures and spirits drawn with a pointed bamboo pen and lampblack ink or Kajal.

Enter Caption

Kohbar- This art style is made on mud walls using natural colours made from vegetables, fruits, leaves of plants mixed with wheat flour or besan. These paintings have their ritual impotance and are usually done on marriage celebrations.

Kohbar

Materials used

Traditionally these were painted on walls using rice paste and vegetable colors on a base of cow dung and mud on walls and floors of huts with a variety of tools including fingers, twigs, brushes, nib pens and matchsticks. The images rarely have spaces or gaps and the edges are usually decorated with geometric and floral motifs. Nowadays Black Gel pens are used for the outline of the drawing. Charcoal and soot is used to make black & white paintings. With time the base of paintings changed to handmade paper, clothes and canvas, still the natural colors were used.

Characteristics of Paintings

The Paintings have a common theme and are usually drawn from religious hindu motifs, including Krushna, Rama, Durga, Lakshmi and Shiva. It is also characterized by eye-catching Geometrical Patterns symbolising love, courage, devotion, prosperity and fertility. The figures in the painting are symbolic, for example, fish depicts good luck and fertility. Topics of paintings include natural elements like fish, birds, animals, turtles, sun, moon, bamboo trees and flowers like Lotus. The paintings depict auspicious occassions like birth, marriage, festivals such as Holi, Durga Puja, Kali Puja, Upanavana and Surya Shashti. Features of this paintings include double line border, bold use of colors, ornate floral patters and exaggerated facial features. Kalakriti in Darbhang vaidehi in Madhubani, Benipatti in Madhubani district and Gram Vikas Parishad in Ranti are some of the major centres of Madhubani Painting which have kept this ancient art form alive.

Madhubani painting skill has been passed on by mostly women to future generations. Previously they were painted on freshly plastered clay walls of the village houses of people on religious occassions. Now they are found on cloth, canvas, paper, paper mache products etc. Madhubani Paintings are done instinctively by artists which makes them unique and exclusive. Madhubani Painting is a folk art and is also used for wall decoration and worship. Pictures of Hindu Gods on trees were drawn and this led to deforestation, preventing trees from being felled. Madhubani Paintings symbols also have conection to Feng Shui. Lotus, fish, turtles, birds found in Madhubani paintings is closely related to the concept of divinity and spirituality in Feng Shui. The Sun has always been a symbol of worship of nature. Most Madhubani houses have paintings of the sun and they worship on daily basis apart from Surya Shashti.

TWO

Color Illustrations

Sun

Pea Hen

Balloon Ride

Radha Krishna

Birds

Swastik

Fish

Lord Ram

The Palm

Peafish

Mother and Daughter

Temple

Sita and Ram Warmala

Parrot

Chicken in an Egg

Tree

Ganeshji

Owl

Lion King and Simba

THREE
HOW TO COLOR

This section contains sketches of all the coloured illustrations. You can choose your favourite medium to colour these sketches like: Sketch pens, Crayons, Pencil Colours, Poster Colours, Waterproof inks, Water Colours, Charcoals if you want to make them black and white, or HB if you want a pencil drawing. You will also find some sketches not exactly the same as the coloured illustrations, it is done so for you to fill out a few patterns and understand them whilst coloring so that when you make your complete painting, you also know all the different kinds of patterns.

Sun

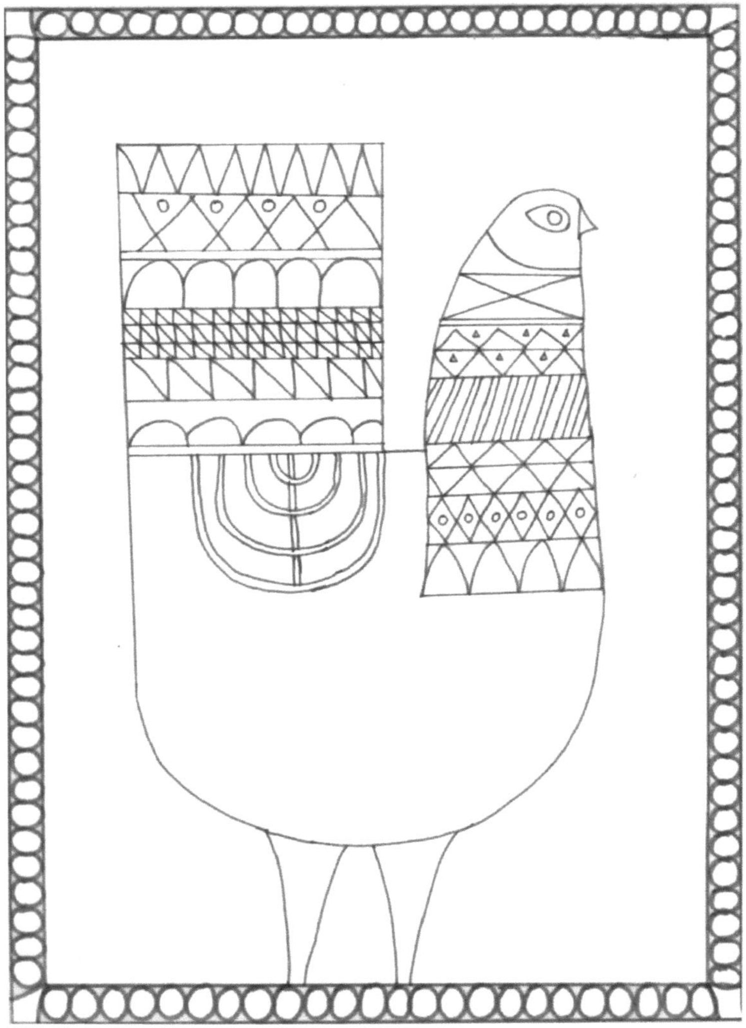

Peahen

Balloon Ride

Radha Krishna

Birds

Peacock

Swastik

Fish

Lord Ram

The Palm

Peafish

Mother & Daughter

Temple

Sita Ram Warmala

Parrot

Chicken in an Egg

Tree

Ganeshji

Owl

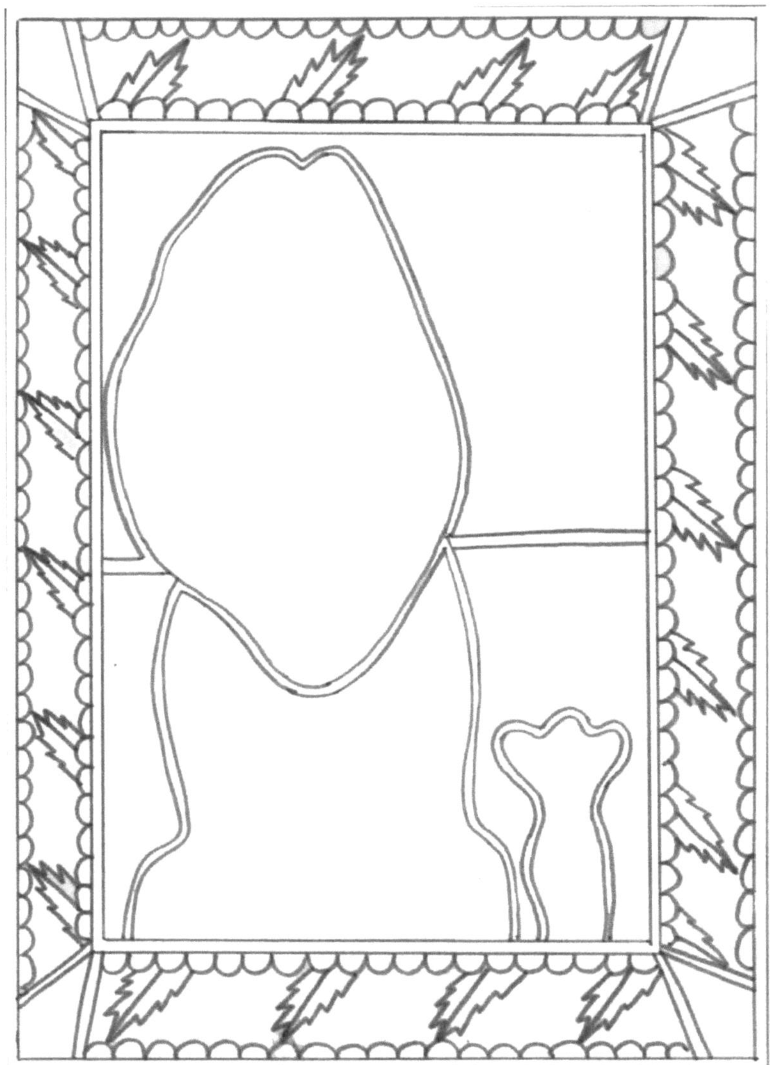

Lion King & Simba

FOUR

How to Draw and Make a Finished Painting

Steps on how to draw your own painting and colour it:

1. Take a plain sheet of white paper or canvas
2. Use a pencil to draw the sketch.
3. With the help of a Black and White Gel Pen trace on the outlline that you have drawn with the pencil. You can then, after the black gel pen ink dries out, erase the pencil lines with the help of an eraser.
4. With your choice of medium of colors you can color the drawing. If you are using paper then water color or water proof inks work best. If you are using a canvas sheet then you can use oil or acrylic colors.
5. You can then frame the painting.

FIVE

Stickers

SIX

Bookmarks

Enter Caption

9 798886 061451

Printed by Libri Plureos GmbH in Hamburg,
Germany